LIFE ON THE REFRIGERATOR DOOR by alice kuipers

MACMILLAN

First published 2007
by Macmillan, an imprint of
Pan Macmillan Limited,
and Macmillan Children's
Books, a division of
Macmillan Publishers Limited
20 New Wharf Road,
London N1 9RR
Basingstoke and Oxford
www.panmacmillan.com

Associated companies throughout
the world

ISBN: 978-0-230-53137-6 (Macmillan)
ISBN: 978-230-53122-2 (Macmillan
Children's Books)

1 3 5 7 9 8 6 4 2

Printed and bound in Great Britain
by Mackays of Chatham plc, Kent

Visit www.panmacmillan.com to read
more about all our books and to buy them.
You will also find features, author interviews
and news of any author events, and you can
sign up for e-newsletters so that you're
always first to hear about our new releases.

To the women in my family,
especially Anneke, Liz, Melanie, Oma, Granny,
and, of course, my mother

This Is Just to Say

I have eaten
the plums
that were in
the icebox

and which
you were probably
saving
for breakfast

Forgive me
they were delicious
so sweet
and so cold

William Carlos Williams

Contents

When I look at you

Hey Claire-Bear,

milk
apples
bananas
avocados
onions
potatoes
tomatoes
mushrooms
carrots and rabbit food for Peter
ground beef
bread
juice – you choose

If you can carry any more, get a chicken and two cans of beans. Don't worry if you can't, I can try and pick these up tomorrow.

Love,

Mom

Money on the counter. Don't forget your key!

Mom,

I bought everything on the list except the chicken and the beans. It was FREEZING outside and carrying the bags back I thought my fingers were going to fall off. I NEED new gloves. We should go to the store again this Saturday – you aren't working this weekend, are you?

Hope you had a good day???

C

I made spaghetti bolognaise for when you get in.

Love,

Mom

I'm running out the door. I'm on call this weekend.
Sorry.

Love,

Mom

I'm going to spend the night at Emma's.

You seemed a bit tired last night, Mom. I hope you're not working too hard???

See you tomorrow.

xox

C

Don't worry, I have my key.

If you get time, could you stop and get a chicken?
I'll cook a Sunday roast tonight.

Love,

Mom

After STARVING TO DEATH FOR AGES I made a chicken thing using a recipe off the Internet. I put the leftovers in the fridge. I waited for you but I figured you weren't EVER going to get back so I just put clingwrap on it. Emma NEVER has to cook for her mom.

I'm going to school early tomorrow so I won't see you. Emma's mom is giving us a ride, she took pity on us with the SNOW. Then I'm babysitting tomorrow night, to make some money so I can buy some of the things I NEED. Like GLOVES. So my hands don't FALL OFF in the COLD!!!!

Why don't you get a cellphone, then at least I could call you????!!!!!!!!

Claire

Dear Claire-Bear,

I had a stressful weekend. It would be nice to come home and not be made to feel guilty.

I hope school was interesting. There's some of the chicken (which was very good, by the way) left over. See you for breakfast. I want to talk to you about something.

Love you,

Mom

I left some money for gloves on the counter.

Claire-Bear,

I had to go. One of my patients delivered two and a half months early. January is a horrible month to have a preemie . . .

When's your presentation? Isn't it coming up soon?

Let's do something tonight. I feel like I haven't seen you for days.

Love you,

Mom

Could you get some more apples?

Hi Mom!

I can't do tonight. I have to go to Emma's to study.
James is coming too and we're all working on the
presentation for tomorrow.

I made some pasta with a cheese sauce so there's no
milk left. I didn't get apples yet.

Hope work was fun. How's last night's baby?

Claire

Could you leave me 10 dollars, Mom?

Hey Claire-Bear,

I picked us up some milk and some more bread.
There's more fruit and veg too. Including apples.

Thanks for the macaroni cheese – very good. You're
a better cook than I am now.

I'm booking you for breakfast on Saturday. I have to
talk to you.

What's the money for?

Mom

Hey Claire-Bear,

Nice to see you last night, if only for a minute. You seemed all grown up when you left. I forget sometimes that you're only fifteen.

I'm sorry: I realize just now that I forgot to ask how your presentation went.

I'll be at work later tonight. Dr Goodman is away and we're all working three times as hard, it seems.

Is Saturday still good for you? We do need to talk properly.

I love you, sweetheart.

Mom

Claire,

Peter's cage needs cleaning. Poor rabbit.

Love,

Mom

Hi Mom!

I got an A!

C

Well done, darling! That's terrific. Was it an important presentation?

MOM!

It was really important. If I EVER saw you I'd be able
to tell you stuff like that. I can't believe you had to ask.

I'm not coming home until late tonight. Emma's parents
asked me for dinner. I might stay over if it keeps
snowing. I'll call to check with you. Tomorrow night
I'm babysitting again.

Claire

Well, Claire, now I feel like a terrible mother. Why don't we try and have a regular night where we talk about everything you've been doing at school. We used to do that, remember?

See you Saturday, we'll talk properly then.

Mom

Claire-Bear, I can't make breakfast Saturday. Let's try for Sunday night.

Could you pick me up some of my moisturizer if you have a minute? I'm all out.

Your father phoned last night. He said to call him.

Love,

Mom

Hi Mom,

I'm studying at Emma's for my test. You forgot my allowance. AGAIN.

C

What did you decide about Sunday night?

Love,

Mom

MOM!

PLEASE PLEASE PLEASE PUT MY ALLOWANCE
OUT!!!!

Hi MOM! (Who I never see any more EVER!)

It's Emma's birthday on Sunday so I'm going to be at her place. I was going to stay at hers tonight too, but Dad asked me to come over so I'm staying at his. He sounded down about something. Any ideas?

I got you a jar of moisturizer. Hope it's the one you like. I think it is, but the store is full of different ones and I couldn't remember. I thought yours was in a white jar, but this one has the right name on a yellow jar. Have they changed it? You need to leave me money next time you want something. Unless you want to increase my allowance . . .

Hope you're OK. You said you wanted to talk to me. Maybe I'll get back from Emma's in time for dinner on Sunday night.

C

Hey Claire-Bear,

How was the weekend with your father? I hope he was
more cheerful in person than on the phone. Maybe
work is stressing him out. He used to get stressed out
about work a lot, but who am I to know?

And how was Emma's birthday?

Claire, honey, I've got a doctor's appointment today.
I've been trying to tell you. It's nothing to worry
about, but I would feel strange if you didn't know.
I found a lump in my right breast. I finally booked
an appointment. I wanted to tell you before I went
to the doctor's, but I suppose I haven't had a chance.
I don't think there's anything to worry about so
please don't think this is more than it is.

I love you, sweetheart.

Mom

Mom!

I can't believe you'd leave me a note telling me something like this!

How are you feeling? How was the doctor's? Should I be worried about you? Is it anything serious? You NEVER go to the doctor's . . .

I have to babysit but I won't be late.

Love and hugs,

Claire

Claire,

I hope I've made you feel better, darling, and you're not so worried. As I told you, the doctor was very nice. I'm going tomorrow afternoon to have the mammogram, just to check that everything's fine – the chance of the lump being anything serious isn't very high.

I suppose being a doctor myself I forget to take my own health as seriously as I should. Anyway, everything will be fine, so please stop worrying. There's really nothing to worry about.

Love,

Mom

Good luck at the doctor's today with your thing.
Sorry I can't come with you, Mom . . .

I have another appointment next week, honey. Do you want to come with me? 4.30 pm Monday – if you could get home from school by 4 we could go over together. See if you can make it.

Love,

Mom

Babysitting tonight, Mom. Gotta run!!!

I can't find my key. Will you be home to let me in?
Call me and let me know.

Are you seeing your father this weekend? Or do you want to do something together?

Hi Mom,

I'll be back later . . . We could watch a movie.

Could you leave me an extra 20 dollars with my
allowance? Pleeeeeeeeaaaaaaaase? I wanted to get
these boots but I haven't got quite enough. I'll cook
ALL NEXT WEEK!

xox

I'm sorry, Mom! I thought I could come with you, but I have this thing at school. Good luck with the doctor! Let me know how it goes . . .

xox

Mom??????

Where are you????

I waited for ages and I thought you'd be home. I
called the hospital, but they said you hadn't come
back to work after your appointment. I even
called Dad to see if he knew anything. Not that he
ever knows where you are.

I'm worried. Should I be? I looked up breast lumps
on the Internet and realized I wasn't sure what I was
looking for, and I suddenly thought that maybe I should
have been taking all this more seriously. If you were
home, I'd probably be less worried . . .

OK. I'm going crazy just waiting for you here. Dad
called – he's taking me for some food. I'll be back soon.
I found my key.

xox

C

GOOD MORNING!!! MOM!

Where are you? What's going on?

It says on your calendar that you'll be at work later today. I'll try and call you there. Why don't you have a cell????

There's cold pizza for breakfast – I brought you the rest of mine. I wish you hadn't just disappeared on me. I know I should have got back quicker from the pizza place, but Dad wanted to talk to me about stuff. Don't worry, I didn't tell him anything.

I'll get home straight after school.

Claire

Hi Claire-Bear,

Sorry to worry you, darling. I went for a long drive.
I'm going back to the doctor's at the end of the week.

Hopefully we'll find out that everything's fine and I'm
worrying over nothing.

I love you. I should be home at around 8.

Someone named Michael called.

Love,

Mom

Hi Mom,

Thanks for your note. Is everything all OK now?

Am at Emma's.

Love and hugs,

Claire

Hey Claire-Bear,

Should we have dinner together tonight? I had to go to work this morning. I notice the world hasn't stopped having babies for little ol' me.

I've just popped out to get some more food for Peter – we're out of everything, including carrots. I'll be back in ten minutes.

Love you,

Mom

Mom,

So we just have to wait until the end of the week and we'll find out everything's fine?

I hate waiting, Mom! Do you remember when we were waiting for the boat that time and we were going to be stuck overnight on that island. Where were we exactly? How old was I?

Oh, I got a B in biology.

See you for dinner.

xox

The meal was lovely last night, Claire. Did you get the recipe for those potatoes from Gran? They were just like hers. And I forgot to tell you – that island was one of the islands of Indonesia. We took you there when you were nine because your father had research to do. It was just before we decided to separate. I'm surprised you remember. It's funny what your children remember of you. I remember that my mom made delicious potatoes and that she used to draw pictures with us when we got home from school.

That Michael called again.

I'll be at work until late. I love you. Try not to worry, OK?

Mom

Sorry your allowance was late.

Should I come with you tomorrow?

C

I'm fine on my own.

See you tonight.

Love,

Mom

Claire,

We need to talk. I'm in my room.

I love you,

Mom

I see the woman
I want to be

I've been sitting with Peter, looking out the window, thinking about how lovely the garden looks, Claire. With the snow starting to melt and Peter's fur full of sun, it doesn't all seem so bad.

I'm sorry, Mom. I had to tell Dad. He knew something was up because I started crying. Please don't be angry with me.

xox

C

Don't worry. We have better things to do than get mad at each other. I've gone over to talk to him.

The clinic called today. They want me to come in tomorrow.

I do love you, darling.

Mom

I'm sorry, Mom. I really didn't mean to yell at you last night. I was just so worried when you went out for that walk and my head filled up with all these ideas of what might happen to you and . . . I can't believe I yelled at you when you have all this going on. I'm really sorry.

Love and hugs,

Claire

It might surprise you, Claire, to know that I remember being fifteen. I'm not so unsympathetic. Your note was nice to read though. Would you like to come with me today – if you get back in time? My appointment is at 4.30 pm. I'll be leaving at 4 sharp. If you can't come today, why don't you come on Friday for the lumpectomy? And after that, everything can go back to normal.

Good job with Peter's cage.

Mom

I'm sorry I missed your appointment, Mom. I can come on Friday though.

Claire

Your allowance is on the counter. We should be ready to leave by 8.15 tomorrow morning.

Love,

Mom

Mom,

I didn't expect it all to be so serious and clean and so real at the hospital. When you wake up, I'm in my room. Come find me . . .

xox

Claire

I'm OK, sweetheart, it wasn't major surgery. Thanks for all those herbal teas . . .

Hi Claire,

Michael called for you. I thought you only went out with him yesterday. Is he someone special?

Nice to see you this morning, darling.

Love,

Mom

Gina called again, Mom. She wants you to call her.

I'll tell you more about Michael later. I've just gone over to Dad's for a bit. He wanted to do something together.

How are you feeling?

Love and hugs,

C

I haven't got time to go to the store, Claire. Could you swing by on your way home from school tomorrow and get:

milk
bread
eggs
fruit – you choose
cucumber and tomatoes
spaghetti – we're completely out

If you have time, could you water the plants too?

I couldn't resist going to work! One of my patients is delivering triplets. Keep your fingers crossed.

Mom

Mom,

I went to the store. See inside the fridge. I watered the plants. I cleaned out Peter's cage. I tidied the sitting room. And the kitchen. And I did the washing up.

I'm going to bed.

Your live-in servant,

Claire

Claire!

I know it's difficult with me out at work all the time, but I used to help my parents around the house too.

Three beautiful babies born last night. Makes the world a better place. I'm feeling very positive. My appointment is next week. They're going to talk about what happens next. I'd like to get it all over with quickly.

x

Mom

Your allowance is on the counter.

MOM!

SORRY WE FOUGHT! I was only saying that I've been doing loads of stuff around the house. Then I feel bad because of everything else that's going on. How are you feeling now?

Claire

Am babysitting.

xox

C

Peter has run out of carrots. Have you got any time to get some? We need bread too.

Mom

Out with Emma.

xox

C

MOM! I can't believe you turned my shirt PINK!
I CAN'T WEAR IT NOW.

I've got the doctor's appointment today. Hopefully it'll be the all-clear.

Love,

Mom

The dishwasher needs emptying.

We had a sad day at work today, Claire. Do you remember the preemie born in January? Maybe you don't, you probably don't, well, I'd been keeping an eye on that one, I suppose she was my little ray of hope through all this. She died this afternoon. She was so tiny.

Feeling a bit low. I'm going for a walk by the river. It wasn't good news yesterday. There seems to be some sort of complication.

Mom

What does 'some sort of complication' mean?
Is everything OK? Why won't you tell me what's
going on?

I'd already arranged to go out with Michael tonight
– I'm really sorry. Don't worry, I PROMISE I won't
be late. I'll be back as soon as possible.

Gina and Marcy called. They're having a dinner party
on the 5th. Call Gina when you get in.

Love and hugs,

Claire

Michael called for you twice.

He sounds nice.

Mom

He is nice! We're going to a movie. See you when I get home?

C

Could you leave me an extra 10 dollars?
Pleeeeeeeaaaaase???

Hope last night was fun, darling. I've gone to Gina's for a bit of female company. I would have preferred yours . . .

x

Mom

Sorry I missed you, MOM! I was babysitting and then I went to Emma's to study. Hope Gina was a good make-up for me. I have a BIG TEST tomorrow and AM KIND OF SCARED!!!!

xox

C

Good luck with your test today, darling. Sorry I'm not here for breakfast. Twin girls on their way right now.

Peter's cage needs cleaning.

See you tonight.

Love,

Mom

Don't forget your key!

I've gone for a jog, Mom, if you're looking for me.
It's a beautiful day and I bet you haven't even had
time to notice. Your crocuses are all out and so
are those little yellow ones that I forget the name
of. They're all smiling in the sun . . .

I feel like we haven't talked about anything for weeks.
I don't even know what the doctor said to you about
treatment stuff. Is everything fine?

My test went OK.

xox

C

You looked tired last night, Mom, I was thinking about it when I went to bed. Should I be more worried than I am about this whole thing? It seems easier sometimes to ask you stuff on paper, like how you're feeling and how things are going with the doctor and stuff.

I'm rushing off to school. Michael's meeting me after so I don't think I'll be home for dinner.

xox

Hi Claire,

Why don't you bring Michael for dinner here one of
these days? We'll have to choose a night when I'm not
on call. It was lonely without you here this evening.
Peter's not a great conversationalist!

I know it's easier to write those questions down. I'm
trying to work out some of the answers.

Love you,

Mom

Nicole called. Did you call her yet?

x

C

I start radiation therapy today so I've gone for that. I'll be going in the mornings from now on.

Mom

Mommy,

When you get up, if you're feeling better, come into the garden. There's pomegranate juice for you in the fridge.

Love and hugs,

Claire-Bear

How are you today, Mom? I just popped over to
Emma's to get the homework I missed. Call if you
need anything . . .

Love and hugs,

Claire-Bear

I'm fine, darling. Thanks for being so concerned.

Mom

I'm just out jogging with Emma, Mom. I'll be back in about forty minutes.

xox

Hi Mom!

Michael and I have gone for a drive. I'll be home in less than an hour.

Nicole called. And Gina too – she'll be here by 6ish and she's bringing dinner.

xox

Morning Claire,

I'm going into work after the radiation today.

By the way: how old is Michael if he's taking you out for a drive? Perhaps we should have a talk about him – you're still only fifteen, Claire.

Your dad called.

Mom

apples
bananas
grapefruit
broccoli
zucchini
salmon
walnuts
avocados
milk
bread
eggs
turkey breasts

I suppose I should start with the super-food diet as soon as possible. Let's hope it helps!? Thanks for getting this, Claire-Bear.

Mom

I'm soooooooooo tired, Mom, so I'm just having a
nap. I got a movie for tonight – To Kill a Mockingbird.
It seemed like one you'd like. It's black and white.

I didn't make it to the store. I'll go tomorrow –
PROMISE.

Peter was soooooooooo cute earlier, you should have
seen him with the toy carrot Dad got him. He called for
you, by the way. Dad – not Peter HAHAHA. (I'm so
tired that I've gone crazy!!!!!!!!)

How was this morning?

Love and hugs and love and stuff,

C

I can't find my key, by the way – have you seen it?

Hi Claire,

I know we both want to be eating healthily, but one night of take-out won't do any harm, right? I ordered Chinese – lemon chicken and chilli beef. I felt like the drive so I've gone to get it.

To Kill a Mockingbird sounds good to me.

I feel a bit shaky. Hopefully some fresh air will make me feel better.

Love and hugs right back at you,

Mom

Claire-Bear,

I had to leave early today for work. I'm a bit behind with things and I kept myself awake worrying about it. Silly – I know. Perhaps I shouldn't be worrying about work so much with everything else going on, but I think I'm going to be fine. We haven't even got a family history, remember.

Good movie, thanks. Thanks for everything you're doing, darling.

Love you,

Mom

Hi Mom,

I've gone jogging. I've left the back door unlocked.

xox

Mom,

Michael said he didn't want to hang out so much. He said—

I don't want to write it. I feel horrible. I'm in the garden. I can't believe he'd do this NOW . . .

xox

Movie night again tonight, Claire-Bear? I'm home
at around 7. I hope last night together made you feel
a little better?

Have a good day, darling. Don't be too hard on
yourself. It's not your fault.

Love,

Mom

Your NEW key is on the counter.

I went for a jog, Mom, if you're wondering where I am.
School was awful today. I couldn't stop thinking about
him. I don't understand what happened? He's so perfect
for me and I thought I was so perfect for him?

See you later. Movie sounds like a good idea – again.
Maybe I should stay in and watch movies with you
forever. Do you think I should call him??? What if
I called him to say that we could be just friends???

C

How was school today? A bit better?

Don't be upset, Claire sweetheart. Let's do something nice this evening. We could fix up Peter's cage. In fact, I'll do that now. I think it's warm enough that we could sit in the garden and have some food. Maybe not. We can eat in the den if you want while watching another movie. Would you like that?

I love you,

Mom

I feel PATHETIC, Mom. I didn't know I'd get so sad about someone. Sorry I've been in such a mood. It's not fair to take it out on you, especially with everything that's been happening – I should have gone with you to your radiation therapy appointments and not just been acting like I was the only person in the world.

I'm out jogging.

Your miserable girl,

Claire

Claire-Bear,

I ran in and ran out. I'll be back in about twenty minutes.

You are most certainly not pathetic. Having your heart broken is tough. It's difficult when a relationship doesn't work out . . . I think if you're writing that you're miserable you're probably better than you were earlier this week – it's like asking for food after you've been down with flu. It's a good sign, darling. You'll feel better soon.

We'll talk when we're both home.

Love,

Mom

Mom,

Could we do something together? Like go to the mall????

New jeans
Flip-flops for summer so that when it gets hot I'm not stuck in sneakers
Swimsuit – probably a bikini, they have a nice one downtown at Isis
Tops
Earrings – Sirens have some nice hoops and they're not expensive

I know it's ages till summer but I'm getting in the mood. Maybe we could plan a vacation or something? OK, I know! I'm only dreaming!

MOM!

I can't believe you think I'm so selfish! I wanted to
go shopping for some new clothes. It doesn't mean I
haven't remembered that you've got things going on
like WORK and your DOCTORS' APPOINTMENTS.
You're being TOTALLY unfair.

Claire

MOM!

You won't talk to me about what's going on with you
so why should I tell you ANYTHING?

Claire

Michael called. I told him you would be back later. Was that the right thing to say? I was a bit surprised to hear from him after you said he told you he wasn't going to call. Hope everything is all right.

Love you, sweetheart.

Mom

Could you please tidy the family room? Your schoolwork is taking over.

Mom!

I've gone out with Michael for a drive!!!!!!

I'll be back later. Don't worry!!!!!!!

Hope everything went well this morning.

xox

Claire

Claire,

I've gone to bed, but I waited up for you. It's a school night. The family room is still a mess.

You'll have to tell me tomorrow what's going on. Where've you been?

Mom

MOM!

Sorry I was so late home, I know it was a school night but it's like the only time EVER. Michael and I got back together. He said he was wrong and he MISSED ME!!!!!

Love and love and more love!!!!!!

Claire

Claire,

I'm going to Gina's.

Take it easy with Michael. There's no rush. You're still young.

Love,

Mom

Mom,

Emma wanted me to come over to help with some homework. I'll be back later. Pleeeeaaaassssseeeeee let's not argue about Michael again, OK? This morning was horrible. I don't see why you have to be so stressed out about it. And I'm not THAT young. You were MUCH younger than Dad when you started dating – so what's the big deal?

Nicole called.

C

Claire,

Last night was dreadful. You're so overwrought I can't talk to you properly. What's happened to my sensible girl?

I didn't say that I didn't like Michael. I haven't even met him – and that's a concern in itself, by the way. I was saying that I was worried about you jumping back in when he seems a little unpredictable. I was saying that I don't like the way he's treated you, which is a reasonable thing to say.

Try not to come home too late tonight.

Mom

I came home and you WEREN'T HERE, Mom. Nothing strange there then, because you're never home, right? Then I get your note on the fridge. If you were here, I'd say this to you, but BECAUSE YOU'RE NOT HERE, I HAVE TO WRITE IT DOWN! Michael's great. He's funny and smart and cute and he's there when I need him, which is more than I can say about you. Or Dad. And talking about Dad, I don't think I need relationship advice from you, Mom!

I'm sick of being sensible. I'm going to stay the night at Emma's.

C

I've had to go for the radiation therapy and then into work for a couple of hours, they couldn't do without me. I think it's very unfair to say I haven't been here when you've needed me.

Be here when I get home.

Mom

I'm staying the night at Emma's again.

Claire

Claire,

What's the point of you having a cellphone if you never switch it on? I had to call Emma's house and her mother said you weren't there. I've been worried sick. Where were you?

I've called school and they've said that you're in your English class. At least I know you're alive. Do you know how ashamed I was to have to tell the receptionist that I was looking for my daughter because I wasn't sure if she was at school? You're out of control, Claire, and I really hope that you didn't spend the night with Michael.

Because I know that you're alive, I'm going to work. Work which pays for all the food we eat and all the clothes we wear and the roof over our heads.

If you're not home when I get home, which will be at 7 pm, then you'll be grounded, Claire. I'll treat you like a little girl if you continue to act like one. Empty the dishwasher when you get in.

Mom

I've gone to Dad's. I didn't spend the night at Michael's. Trust you to think the worst.

Claire

I love you, Claire, but you're behaving in a way I can't tolerate.

I spoke to your father last night and he said that you were coming to the house to pick up some things because you're staying with him. I can't believe you're doing this, Claire. Running to your father to deal with our conflict is very disappointing and very childish, which proves my point that you're too young to be seeing anyone seriously.

Michael called twice this evening. What's going on with you?

Mom

I'll be at Dad's if you need me.

Claire

Dad and I are going to Grandpa's for the night. I came by to pick up some stuff.

Claire

Mom,

I watched a DVD last night for the families of someone who has breast cancer (Emma got it for me from the library). This is hard to write, but I think we need to talk about this more. Dad said maybe we've been fighting so much because we haven't been talking enough. I'm not sure if I should be worrying about you or if I should be just getting on with my life. You're making out like it's no big deal so maybe I should be doing that too.

Am I making too much of it all, Mom? I'm staying here tonight.

Claire

Claire,

There isn't a book with rules written in to tell me how to live my life or how to handle all this. I wish there was.

You have school, and a relationship, and things to do that any normal fifteen-year-old should be doing. When this is all better, we can go back to how things were.

I'm glad you've decided to spend some time at home. I've just gone for a walk by the river. Let's talk when I get back.

Love,

Mom

Is there something I don't know, Mom? You seemed distracted last night. I'm sorry about all the fights we've had.

Mom,

Please talk to me.

Claire

I just can't, Claire. I'm sorry but I just can't.

Be patient.

Mom

Dearest Claire,

If I get sicker then I want you to go and live with your father. It's not that I don't love you. Please don't ever think that.

Love,

Mom

Mom,

I'm shaking as I write this. I've just walked into an empty house – none of the lights were on. The kitchen was empty and I see a note stuck to the fridge door with that magnet I gave you – the one with a picture of me as a baby on it. Did you realize when you wrote your last note that you'd used it?

I noticed the plant in the corner, the cactus which almost reaches the ceiling. I don't remember it being so tall. And then I read your note.

People get better from this all the time. I'm really trying to be strong for you, but you have to remember you'll be OK, Mom – you have to be. You'll be OK.

Claire

Mom,

I just found your letter to me in the garbage. Why did you throw it away? Why didn't you tell me what was going on? Is it really bad?

I'm sorry that we've been fighting so much. Are you OK?

Claire

Claire,

I'll be home at around 6 tonight. When you get this note, perhaps you could just wait for me.

How could I tell you? I've hardly begun thinking about getting better and other things start going on. It doesn't normally happen like this – I know, I've seen women go through it. And then you weren't here because we were having a stupid disagreement. Oh Claire, I've been so foolish about this whole thing. Your note the other week, the one when you told me you'd just watched the DVD for families of breast-cancer sufferers, do you know that I wept for an hour after reading that? Do you know that this is the first time I've really admitted to myself that I have breast cancer? Me, I have breast cancer. I really do. And it's not getting better.

I've been too weak to admit that I need you. I didn't want this to interfere with your life, I didn't want you to have to change what you were doing or stop being my little girl.

I don't want your dad to know about this development. Not just yet. Not until I get my feet back on the ground.

I love you,

Mom

Strong and brave

I found a book for you, Mom. It's poetry by other survivors. Perhaps you'd like to write some poetry or paint or do something creative. It might be good for you. I know it's weird right now, but we should be hopeful, right? That's what the book says.

You're so strong. Even as a little girl I knew that you were the strongest out of all the moms, and the fastest. Do you remember you always used to run the fastest on school sports days?

You were twenty-eight when you had me. I wonder what you were like when you were fifteen. I wonder if we would have been friends at school. I bet we would.

Summer seems to have snuck up on us. It's sunny today. The sun is filling the kitchen and it makes me more hopeful. I know you'll be fine, Mom. I just know it.

I love you and I'm sorry about the last month and all that stuff with Michael. I'm sorry I went to stay with Dad. I don't know what came over me. It seems so silly now.

I'll be home at 5. I made coffee. Decaffeinated!

I do think we should tell Dad what's going on.
And Gina.

C

Thanks for the book, darling.

I've gone to lie down.

Mom

Could you take the garbage out?

I'll call at lunchtime. Two more weeks of school!
Then it's SUMMER!!!!

C

I need some flip-flops!

How did it go at the doctor's today, Mom? I wish you'd let me come with you. I called but you weren't home. I'm hoping that you went for a long drive and that they just have it all wrong.

I'm in the garden with Peter. Sitting in the sun. Feeling strange.

Claire

I came in and I read your note and I went to the back door and I looked at you in the garden and I couldn't tell you, Claire. How can I tell you that life isn't as good as it should be? I'll fight this thing. I'll fight it. But I can't get up the strength to tell you face to face what the doctor said. I'm sorry.

I'm lying down.

Mom

You looked so small in your room last night, Mom.
Oh God, I can't believe this is happening. I don't
understand how everything has happened so quickly.
I thought that everything would be fine. I thought that
this only happened to other people. I have a friend at
school whose grandmother survived. She ate lots of
broccoli and did lots of exercise. Like you do. You'll
be fine. AND YOU'RE MUCH YOUNGER THAN
MY FRIEND'S GRANDMOTHER!!!!!!

I believe in you, Mom. You'll be fine. I'll see you
at noon.

Claire

When you get in, Claire, call your dad's cell. He's going to drive you to meet me at the doctor's. We have to talk about this together, all of us.

I'm not sure that you believing in me is going to fix this, Claire-Bear, and perhaps neither is broccoli or exercise. I'm sorry, darling. Let's all listen to the doctor together and work something out.

Love,

Mom

We can't give up hope, Mom. Lots of people recover from this. And think of all the things you still have left to do! All those babies to deliver. Me to look after.

The surgery and the chemo will help. You'll get better, I know it.

Broccoli and exercise this evening. We'll walk along the river together. We can look at those pink flowers that you like – what are they called? We can stand at the edge of the water and watch the sun tumbling down. I'll hold your hand through this, Mom. See you at 4?

Love and hugs,

Claire

All right, Claire. I just have to get something from Nicole. And, yes, I will tell her that we need some help.

A walk will be lovely. Exercise and broccoli. As you say, darling.

Mom

Could you get some bread and milk, please, Claire?

Mom

Emma called.

Mom

I have to babysit tonight but I'll be back as soon as I'm done. LAST DAY OF SCHOOL TOMORROW!!!! YAY!!!!! YAY!!!!!!!!!!!!!!!!!

C

Claire,

I've gone to lie down.

James from school called.

Love,

Mom

Michael called, sweetheart. He can't make it tonight.
He said to call him.

Hope everything's OK?

Mom

Why is this happening to you, Mommy? Why is it happening so fast? Everything was fine at Christmas.

I'm in the back bedroom on the Internet, trying to understand what the surgery is going to be like. Everything's fine with Michael. He found me talking about it all a bit depressing, I guess. I shouldn't have tried to talk to him. He didn't even know anything anyway!

It doesn't seem real???? Does it???

Love and hugs,

Claire

Hi darling,

I can only deal with the facts, Claire. I thought I could go to work <u>and</u> deal with the awful radiation therapy. But it was really tough, and I wish I'd talked to you about how terrible it made me feel. I'm not used to being on this side of the doctor's desk, remember? Doctors are the worst patients.

Then it was taken out of my hands. Because I'm not in control, Claire. I can't control this, and that's what's really frightening.

We should take notes next time we go to the doctor's. You can be my note taker.

I have to go and rest. I'll see you later.

I'm ready for tomorrow.

Love,

Mom

I've made you some chicken soup, Mom.
How are you feeling?

When you get up, Mom, I'm just in the garden.
I'm reading another book of poetry written by other
people who've been where you are. One writer says
that losing a breast makes you feel less of a woman.
It's hard for me to understand because I find it hard to
think of you like that, Mom, as the sort of woman who
feels like a woman and not like a mom. Does that make
any sense? Can you talk to me about these things? I'm
trying to be more grown up but it's REALLY hard.

I won't be outside for long and I'll come and check
on you, so if you don't feel like coming to get me then
I promise I'll be in your room with you soon.

Love and hugs,

Claire

Morning Mom!

I've just gone with Dad to get you a hat (just in case). He said he'd seen a beautiful one but he wanted me to check it out with him.

You're doing well, Mom. I'm proud of you. You'll be back at work before you know it – back to your usual self in no time.

Dad thought he might stay around this evening. I hope that's no problem???

Hugs and love,

Claire

I have my key.

I'm sorry I got so angry with you, Claire. I'm doing the best I can. First I have to deal with the after-effects of the surgery, then I'll think about the chemo. After that I can focus on getting better.

Mom

I'm with Michael – he's driving me to take back the hat. I'm sorry, Mom. Dad and I didn't mean to upset you. I know that you still have your hair and that you might not lose it. I was trying to cheer you up.

You'll feel better soon. There's still some soup in the fridge.

Claire

Emma and James and I are outside in the garden. They came over to see if they could do anything to help around the house. Sweet!!!!

Come and look for us. It might cheer you up to sit in the sun????

Claire

I'm sorry that Emma and James were here, Mom. I thought it would be nice to have some company, but I'll ask next time I want to have friends over, OK?

You look beautiful to me.

Love and hugs,

Claire

I'm sorry, Claire. I didn't expect to feel so dreadful. I feel a little stronger now, but this kind of knocked me for six. At least I'll only lose my right breast once (that was supposed to be a joke, but it's not really very funny). It's nice of you to tell me that I look beautiful. I certainly don't feel beautiful. I feel like I'm underwater and I can't work out how to swim to the surface. I'm a bit lost, that's all. I don't want you to worry about me.

The chemo starts soon. Maybe you could come with me?

As for my hair, I'll keep my fingers crossed.

Mommy

When I look at you
I see the woman I want to be
Strong and brave
Beautiful and free

Claire

P.S. I love you

Things have happened so fast, Claire-Bear. I feel like I've lost control of everything and when I look at myself I don't recognize who I am any more. Is this what life is?

I'm sorry, I don't mean to burden you. You're only fifteen.

I'll make breakfast for you when I get back. I'll be ten minutes.

Love,

Mom

Claire,

Sorry I forgot your allowance. It's on the counter.
There's an extra 10 dollars with it, honey.

Love,

Mom

James called. He said to call him.

xx

Mom

Mom,

Am eating breakfast but can't find you. I'll be in the garden.

I wrote this list for Dad and wrote a copy for you. BUT ONLY BECAUSE YOU ASKED FOR IT!

Birthday List:

Books – I like Sylvia Plath
Make-up
Jewellery
iPod
Laptop instead of our ANCIENT desktop.
Clothes, or gift voucher for Isis . . .

Nearly sixteen!!!!

MOM!

Maybe Emma and James could come this weekend
and perhaps I could ask some of my other friends too.
Cheryl and Juliette and Alison and Ellie, maybe Jim,
Sandy and Jack? And maybe Michael too?????!!!!!!!
We could hang out here and have a bar-be-que (HOW
DO YOU SPELL THAT??? BAR B Q? BBQ?????)

What about Saturday? Are you up for it? Or we
could all go to Dad's and you could come and then
you wouldn't have to cook?

HAPPY BIRTHDAY TO YOU
HAPPY BIRTHDAY TO YOU
HAPPY BIRTHDAY DEAR CLAIRE
HAPPY BIRTHDAY TO YOU

Happy birthday, my beautiful, brave daughter. I can
hardly believe that it was sixteen years ago that you
were a tiny, perfect baby. I remember hearing your first
cry. You were a miracle.

Peter and I are in the garden. We'll be having breakfast
out here (he'll only be having carrots and seeds
probably – I'm having salmon on a bagel . . . I have
an extra one for you). What a beautiful summer we're
having.

Love you, birthday girl.

Mom

Thanks for the breakfast and everything this morning, Mom. I love ALL MY PRESENTS! Best of all was seeing you outside.

That dress looked lovely on you.

Claire

Once chemo starts tomorrow, I won't be going in the sun. Did you know that, darling? The sun reacts badly with the chemicals, apparently, so I've been sitting in the garden enjoying the sun on my skin for a little bit of this morning.

I can't believe how many pills I have to take. And, worse, I'm not sure if chemotherapy is a good thing. Just the word makes it sound frightening.

Mom

I'm sorry about this Saturday, Claire. I know you were looking forward to having your friends here. I feel terrible about it all.

Love,

Mom

Don't apologize, Mommy. I should be the one saying sorry. I wish I hadn't given you such a hard time over Michael in the spring. Is it my fault? Is all this my fault?

Claire

It's no one's fault, Claire. It's just how life is sometimes.
Maybe it's my fault for trying to protect you when your
father and I divorced. I didn't want you to ever see that
the world can be a bad place, that life is difficult, that
sometimes we can't control our destinies.

This is not your fault, Claire. This is nobody's fault.
Sometimes there just isn't anyone to blame.

We haven't talked about Michael very much. I know
you're still seeing him. How is that going? I won't be
angry.

Love,

Mom

Emma called.

We're out of milk – money on the counter.
(With your allowance and your key – it was
under the kitchen table.)

Hey Mom,

I'm worried that something's wrong with me. My heart feels like it's beating too fast. I feel like all the colours in the room have got more intense. I mean, blue is more blue somehow and red is more red, and yellow suddenly looks like the sun is shining. I don't think I'm making much sense, sorry! I just have a funny sensation. It's as if I've eaten too much food and my stomach is unpleasantly full. Writing it down is making me feel worse, actually. What's wrong with me? Maybe I need to get out of the house?????

Do you want to go on vacation somewhere when the chemo's finished? Not somewhere expensive, but maybe we could take the car (we could leave Peter with Dad) and we could just drive somewhere. Road-trip girls . . .

Talking of Peter, his ear seems to be squashed up – has he hurt himself, do you think?

Love and hugs,

Claire

Claire,

What you were describing, that feeling, it sounds a bit like anxiety. We could take you to the doctor's if you want. But please don't worry, darling, everything's going to be OK.

I can beat this thing.

And we'll talk about a vacation later. I can't think about that now. It would be like being at the end of a road when I haven't driven along it yet.

Peter's ear looks fine to me.

Love,

Mom

Dear Claire,

My heart is all fluttery, like I've got a hummingbird
trapped inside. I've gone to lie down.

Mom

I've just remembered, your allowance was on the counter with the money for bread and milk the other day.

Are you still feeling anxious?

Mom

James called. He said he'd try again later.

Love,

Mom

Am with Emma. Back by 9.30.

xox

Claire

Poor Claire,

It's not been much of a summer vacation, has it?

I'll make it up to you. One day.

Mom

I don't need a summer vacation. I just want you to get better.

Love and hugs,

Claire

Michael called. He can't make it tonight.

Love,

Mom

It's so hot today, I've gone to lie down.

Love,

Mom

Michael called. Call him when you get in.

All OK?

Love,

Mom

Kept a smile on my face all day to think of you dancing in the kitchen this morning, Claire. The edges of the grass are turning brown and poor Peter is gasping in the heat, but you're cool and fresh and dancing.

Love,

Mom

Beautiful and free

Hey Mom,

You looked so brave in the hospital. I wondered what it felt like to be you, what it felt like to have that stuff going into your body. I know it felt strange for me. I mean, you're the one who's the grown-up, yet I was trying to look after you.

I didn't tell you, but the nurse came to talk to me. She gave me a couple of books. We could read them together???

Love and hugs,

Claire

Hi Claire,

Hope your first day in Grade 11 was great and that you and Emma have lots of classes together again this year. Leftover pasta and salad in the fridge, and I bought you a slice of cappuccino cake from the bakery as a special treat.

I had to lie down for a while.

Mom

Hi Mom,

Gina and Nicole are coming over tonight to bring us
dinner, and they'll do it every time we need it while the
chemotherapy goes on so that you can rest. Gina asked
me about it a couple of weeks ago and I told her we
were managing. But when she asked again, I thought
it might be nice to have company.

Is that OK?

C

Fine.

Mom

Is there anything you want, Mom?

Write it down.

C

To feel better.

Mom

I've been writing some poetry and Miss Manda liked it. I'll show you some, if you like. And I feel less worried than I have done. I've gone out with Emma just for a short while. I'll be back by 6 at the latest, promise!

Gina will be here before me. We're having lasagne tonight. YAY!

Claire

How's your arm feeling today, Mom? Should we call the hospital and ask them about it?

Love and hugs,

Claire

Hi Claire,

I think I'm going to need a hat. Did you take that pretty blue one back in the end?

I'm lying down.

Mom

When the road bends
We'll be on it together,
Taking the curve
Clinging
To each other, like mother
To daughter,
To mother.

Miss Manda said the school magazine will publish this
one. Maybe I'd like to be a writer when I grow up.

Claire

I loved the poem, sweetheart.

I'm not feeling up to the drive today. I was fine this morning, but I'm worn down now.

Next batch tomorrow. I'm not sure I can bear it. I feel sick just thinking about it.

Mom

James called.

I'll come with you.

Love you,

Claire

I'm glad it's not so hot, honey. I know you love the summer, but it's nice when the weather starts to turn . . . Soon the leaves will be in full colour.

Your allowance is on the counter.

Mom

It's early in the morning, Claire, and I've been sitting here thinking for a long time. I've been thinking about you and me, and your father. It seems that since we separated you've had to grow up a whole lot more than I ever gave you credit for. Think of all the shopping you've done, and cooking, and now you're looking after me. I know Gina is helping, but really you've been so supportive to me, and I wonder if I've done enough for you in the past.

Have I been a good mother? It's the sort of question every mother wants to ask but often they don't get the chance. Or they don't dare.

I love you,

Mom

Mom,

I don't know what to say. You're my mother and all I want is for you to get better. Perhaps I'm not as grown up as you think.

I'm just taking a walk. Michael called and when I told him I was busy today he was disappointed so we're going out for a bit. I'll be back in time.

Love and hugs,

Claire

MOM!

You should have waited for me. I was here in time!
Now you're at the hospital all alone and I'm stuck
here climbing the walls.

I wish you'd stop and think sometimes. It doesn't make
it easier for me when you do stuff like this and I can't
even get mad at you because you're sick.

I'm sitting with Peter in the garden.

Claire

Gina told me that she drove you home yesterday. She's going to stay the night here tonight and I'm going to Dad's. I think it's a good idea.

I hope you're feeling OK, Mom.

Claire

Gina told me that you went to the Rose Bush Store without me. She said they helped fit you for a bra and that she even heard you laugh. I'm staying at Dad's again.

Claire

Hi Mom,

I'm back from Dad's. I realized when I got there that I wasn't handling this right.

I'm sleeping here tonight.

Love and hugs,

Claire

Claire-Bear,

I'm sorry. I've been acting like I'm the only one in the world – like you don't need me to be there for you, and that I don't need you to be there with me. I do need you, darling, I'm just finding it hard to make the transition from being a single mother, a woman who relied on nobody for help, to a half-woman who needs her daughter to look after her.

The doctor gave me the details of a group of local women who have survived breast cancer, or who have it themselves still, like me, and Gina took me yesterday. You wouldn't believe how many other women go through this, how many women who live round here have the same problems. One woman is only thirty and her daughter is six years old. She knows that she's dying and she's in despair. She held my hand and told me I had to be strong for you, I have to include you. I held her thin fingers and she squeezed tightly. 'Don't waste time,' she said.

She's right, Claire, I have to talk to you. I have to open myself up and I have to treat you like an adult. I've been holding back to keep you young and sunny and full of light, but I've been doing you a disservice. If I let you be a grown-up then you'll be one, and I have to be able to do that.

I've been feeling very low and very frightened. I've been wondering what my life has been about. All those years I assumed I had to live my dreams, but it seems that those years are behind me now, that I've had my time and that I've wasted it somehow, that I've missed the point. I have you, my darling girl – having you has given my life meaning and joy beyond compare. But what about all the other things I wanted to do? I've never been to Africa. I've never read Proust. I've never learned to play the piano or even read music – those black blobs on the page that people can translate into beautiful sounds are a mystery to me and they may always be. I've never skydived, I've never seen the desert, I've never been fishing.

I know it's not all bad news, and there is hope, but I have to let myself think about the alternative, and when you smile and tell me broccoli and exercise I feel exhausted, simply exhausted. I'm not without hope, I'm just trying to think it all through.

I'm tired, really tired, and I don't feel very well today.

I've told you as much as I can for now.

I love you,

Mom

Hi Mom,

There were a lot of things in your letter that I found hard to read. I wanted to read about all the things you HAVE done in your life but instead you wrote about things you haven't. And I realized I hardly know about your life. What were you like when you were my age? What did you and Dad used to talk about? Where did you two meet? Did you only marry him because you were pregnant with me? Why did you two divorce? Has it been hard to bring me up alone?

All these questions are making me cry, Mom, and I don't know why. Perhaps they're opening up a world I'm only just starting to see the edges of. An adult world. It's scary and I don't like it.

Michael and I haven't been getting on so well. He's not as great as I thought he was. Don't worry about me, but I think I'm going to break up with him. Emma agrees. She says he's HORRIBLE and I should never have got back with him!

Love and hugs, Mommy,

C

Sometimes you look so much like my mother, Claire. I don't know if I've ever told you that.

The support meeting is this evening. I forgot to tell you at breakfast. I'll heat up the casserole Nicole made and we'll go together.

Did I answer all your questions?

Love,

Mom

I think the idea of making a photo album is great,
Mom. I didn't know we had so many family photos!

Let's start this evening.

Thanks for bringing me to the group last night. I feel
less alone – do you know what I mean?

Love and hugs,

Claire

I had so much fun, Claire. I wish I could be sitting at the kitchen table with you cutting out photographs forever. I'm looking forward to tonight.

Should we put some of your poems among the photographs?

Dishwasher needs emptying.

Love,

Mom

Hi Mom!

I'm still laughing at the photograph of Peter sitting on your head. I wish I could remember that day!

I know that you might not get better, Mom – although it's incredibly hard to write, I do understand that and I know why we had to talk about it last night. It would be the hardest thing in the world, but I don't want you to worry about me. You've given me strength to face the future.

I will hope for the best while preparing for the worst, Mom. Does that seem like a good compromise?

Love, strength, light, and hugs,

Claire

I just wish I hadn't left it so long before I went to the doctor in the first place. I keep thinking maybe none of it would be so bad if I'd gone straight away. I wish I'd been more responsible, Claire, more like I would have been if I'd been a better mother.

Even the doctor says it's unusual. It's not your fault.

And I don't want a 'better mother'. I have you.

I'm making a list for Gina, Mom. What else do we need?

eggs
peanut butter
fruit
soya milk
orange juice
bread
cheese

We're out of olive oil and vinegar. Some salad greens would be nice.

How are you today? Thinking of you, Mommy.

See you later

xox

Last night was fun, Mom! It was nice to see you smiling!

xox

Claire, darling,

I'm feeling a little out of breath. I'm going to see the doctor again tomorrow.

James called. He asked how I was. I had to hold back tears. He seems very sweet.

Mom

Claire, darling,

I'm spending the night at the hospital. I told your dad.
He'll bring you to see me later.

I love you,

Mom

Claire,

I'll be spending another couple of nights at the hospital. Gina brought me here to collect a few things. Could you clean Peter's cage before you come tonight? He's looking a bit forgotten.

I don't know where the future will take us, but I know you'll be OK.

I couldn't have a more fabulous daughter.

I love you,

Mom

I couldn't have a more fabulous Mom.

Love,

Claire

I've made your room really nice for you. If I'm not here when you get here, I'm just getting Peter some carrots.

l love you

Dearest Mom,

I went to the support group today and Mary suggested I write to you even though you won't be able to read it. She said it might make me feel closer to you and there might be things I wished I could say to you.

I came to our house to write it and I'm sitting at the kitchen table. The house is going to be sold soon, but right now I can almost pretend that you're lying in your room, or you're out at work and I'm waiting for you to get back so you can tell me about the babies you delivered, or just give me a hug. The worst part about coming here was that I looked on the fridge door for a note from you, and there wasn't one. The door was white and empty. I cried for ages.

I miss you, Mom. I wish you were still here with us. I like living with Dad but I wish that you were still here. I don't understand why you had to be taken from me, or why you got sick, or how you died so quickly when other women survive this all the time. How could it happen like this? How could you just leave? How could you leave me? It's like I'm mad at you, Mom. How dumb is that?

Do you remember how pretty fall was, how we looked out your bedroom window as you got sicker and watched the yellows and reds brighten the sky? You tried so hard to fight it, Mom. I hate that it was so hard for you.

Winter was long and cold. I've been going to school, but I feel like I'm in a fog most of the time. Emma's been sweet, so has James, and Gina has been great, Mom, you wouldn't believe. But they're not you. Christmas was awful.

Mary's right. I do feel better writing to you, although it's making me cry more than I have in months. She says it's OK to be sad, and angry, and confused. It doesn't feel OK. Not at all.

I suppose I should tell you that Peter's fine. I've set up his cage at Dad's, and when I sit and stroke him I remember our summer and fall together, making those photograph albums, eating dinners that Gina cooked, getting to know each other better. I can try and make myself forget about how hard it was for you at the end, but I'll never forget how strong you were and how brave. I have a picture of you in a wheelchair at the hospital. Your eyes are so big and beautiful. You look surprised, Mom, like you were caught out. I feel like we were both caught out.

I wish we'd had more time, Mom. I guess that's all I have to say really. I wish I'd had more time with you. But I'm glad of the time we did have. So glad. When I get back to Dad's, I'm going to look at the albums and remember it all.

I think I'll leave this letter for you here. In this empty kitchen. So you'll know if you come home that I love you and I miss you. Please don't worry about me.

Your daughter,

Claire

Dearest Mom,

It's my birthday tomorrow. I can't believe I'm going to be seventeen already! Dad and James (he's my boyfriend now – you remember James from school?) have got some sort of surprise planned, but I have to pretend I don't know what's going on. I'll act surprised.

I kept the key from our house with me, waiting for the right moment. Today I was sitting by the river where we used to walk and I suddenly knew what to do with it. I threw it as hard as I could. It glinted in the sun, then it tumbled into the water and was gone. I felt good, Mom, for the first time in a long time, I felt good. Sitting by the water, I thought I could hear your voice in the wind, telling me you were OK.

One day I'm going to fold this note up and put it in the river. For now I'll keep it close to me.

I love you,

Claire

Thank you to Marguerite Buckmaster,
whom I never had time to meet

If you have been affected by any of the issues raised in this book, contact Breast Cancer Care. Breast Cancer Care is the UK's leading provider of breast cancer information, practical assistance and emotional support. Anyone with breast cancer or breast health concerns can get free, confidential support and information from the Breast Cancer Care helpline on 0808 800 6000 or from the website at www.breastcancercare.org.uk